Mark Cuban

MARK CUBAN

Disrupting the Status Quo-From Garbage Bags to Billions

Debra C. Lee

Mark Cuban

All rights reserved. No part of this publication may be reproduced, distributed, or transmitted in any form or by any means, including photocopying, recording, or other electronic or mechanical method, without the prior written permission of the publisher, except in the case of brief quotations embodied in critical reviews and certain other noncommercial uses permitted by the copyright law.
Copyright © Debra C. Lee, 2024.

Mark Cuban

TABLE OF CONTENTS

INTRODUCTION

CHAPTER 1: WHO IS MARK CUBAN

Early life and upbringing

CHAPTER 2: ENTREPRENEURIAL BEGINNINGS

The Initial Attempts

Cuban's Methodology for Small Enterprises

Errors and First Teachings

CHAPTER 3: THE ROAD TO BUSINESS SUCCESS

Gaining Knowledge in Business

MicroSolutions

Important Obstacles and Successes

The CompuServe Sale

Getting Started in Broadcasting

CHAPTER 4: BILLION-DOLLAR SUCCESS

Knowledge Acquired from the Dot-Com Boom

Increasing Investment Diversification

CHAPTER 5: DISRUPTING INDUSTRIES

Technology and Media

CONCLUSION

Mark Cuban

INTRODUCTION

Mark Cuban is one of the few people in the world of entrepreneurship and business innovation who embodies the spirit of success and disruption. Cuban's journey from modest beginnings delivering trash bags door-to-door in Pittsburgh, Pennsylvania, to becoming a wealthy investor, Dallas Mavericks owner, and a well-known personality on "Shark Tank," is quite amazing.

Following his graduation from the University of Pittsburgh with a degree in business administration, Cuban set out on a career that would disrupt entire industries and question accepted knowledge. He started his first business, MicroSolutions, specializing in software sales and consulting, and made a name for himself as a shrewd businessman who could see trends in the market.

Mark Cuban

But it was Cuban's audacious entry into the rapidly developing internet space that thrust him into the public eye. He co-founded Broadcast.com, a trailblazing streaming media startup, with Todd Wagner. After the company achieved ground-breaking success and was acquired by Yahoo! for billions of dollars, Cuban's reputation as a tech visionary and billionaire entrepreneur was cemented.

Beyond his commercial accomplishments, Mark Cuban's ownership of the Dallas Mavericks NBA team has made the team a consistent challenger and won him a great deal of praise for his meticulous nature and dedication to perfection.

In addition to examining the significant moments in Cuban's career, "Mark Cuban: Disrupting the Status Quo - From Garbage Bags to Billions" delves into the ideas and precepts that have shaped his path. This biography allows readers to explore the mind of a maverick who continues to question the status quo and inspire future generations of entrepreneurs through in-depth

Mark Cuban

interviews, personal tales, and insights into his business practices.

Mark Cuban

CHAPTER 1: WHO IS MARK CUBAN

American investor, entrepreneur, and television personality Mark Cuban is well-known. The Dallas Mavericks, an NBA basketball franchise, are owned by him, and that is probably how most people know him. Cuban, who was born in Pittsburgh, Pennsylvania, on July 31, 1958, showed an entrepreneurial flair at a young age by going door-to-door as a teenager and selling trash bags.

Cuban's career took off during the late 1990s dot-com boom when he co-founded the internet radio startup Broadcast.com, which Yahoo! eventually purchased for billions of dollars. Because of his success, he became one of the world's wealthiest people and was able to diversify his holdings by investing in media companies, sports teams, and technological startups, among other industries.

Mark Cuban

In addition to being the Dallas Mavericks' owner since 2000, Cuban has made appearances as a "shark" investor on the well-liked reality TV program "Shark Tank," where entrepreneurs present their ideas to a panel of affluent investors in the hopes of receiving funding.

Mark Cuban, who is well-known for his candor, original ideas, and support of technology and entrepreneurship, is still a major player in the entertainment and business industries.

Early life and upbringing

On July 31, 1958, Mark Cuban was born in Pittsburgh, Pennsylvania, to Norton and Shirley Cuban. His mother held several occupations, including retail, while his father was an automobile upholsterer. In the Mount Lebanon suburb, Cuban was raised in a middle-class family and went to Mount Lebanon High School.

Mark Cuban

Cuban showed a strong sense of entrepreneurship and a flair for business at a young age. He began selling trash bags door-to-door when he was twelve years old, and he experienced his first taste of success when he was able to afford the high-end basketball shoes he had always desired. His passion for business was ignited by this early encounter, which also laid the groundwork for his future pursuits.

Cuban's entrepreneurial spirit persisted throughout his adolescence. In addition to running newspaper routes and selling stamps and coins, he also worked as a bartender. These early endeavors taught him a great deal about customer service and sales techniques in addition to giving him financial independence.

Cuban enrolled at the University of Pittsburgh to study business after finishing high school. He showed his entrepreneurial spirit even as a college student, planning disco parties and giving dancing classes to supplement his income. His business and finance career began during his tenure at the University of Pittsburgh.

Mark Cuban

After graduating, Cuban started working in a variety of industries, such as consulting and software sales. Eventually, he established MicroSolutions, a computer consulting business with a focus on system integration and software sales, in Dallas, Texas. Cuban sold MicroSolutions to CompuServe in 1990 for $6 million, capitalizing on the company's quick success thanks to his astute business sense and unwavering work ethic.

After MicroSolutions was sold, Cuban started a new phase of his career concentrating on investments and technology businesses. His major break came when he and Todd Wagner founded Broadcast.com in 1995. As the first website to stream media over the internet, Broadcast.com expanded rapidly to become a multi-million dollar business. Cuban became a wealthy businessman when he and Wagner sold Broadcast.com to Yahoo! in 1999 for $5.7 billion in Yahoo! stock.

In addition to his commercial endeavors, Mark Cuban is well-known for being the owner of the Dallas

Mark Cuban

Mavericks, an NBA basketball franchise he acquired in 2000. The Mavericks have had tremendous success under his ownership, including the 2011 NBA Championship.

Mark Cuban's extraordinary career as an investor, business magnate, and entrepreneur began with his early years and upbringing. His early hustle and selling skills gave him a strong work ethic and an acute awareness of business operations. Cuban has made a lasting impact on the entertainment and technology sectors with his lifelong innovations and boundary-pushing. His journey from door-to-door garbage bag sales to becoming a multibillionaire investor and owner of a sports franchise is a credit to his fortitude, tenacity, and spirit of entrepreneurship.

CHAPTER 2: ENTREPRENEURIAL BEGINNINGS

Mark Cuban's sense of entrepreneurship was apparent from an early age. Cuban was born in Pittsburgh, Pennsylvania, on July 31, 1958, and was raised in a working-class household. His mother Shirley worked at a variety of odd jobs, and his father Norton Cuban was an automobile upholsterer. His commercial pursuits would be built around the virtues of hard work and tenacity that his family instilled in him.

When Cuban was twelve years old, he decided to start his own business to afford a pricey pair of basketball shoes. He went to his father for a loan to buy trash bags in bulk, which he subsequently sold door to door, rather than asking his parents for money. He learned valuable lessons about customer service, profit margins, and sales from this early experience.

During his teenage years, Cuban never stopped looking for ways to make money. He used his expertise and love of collecting to sell coins and stamps. All of his endeavors, no matter how minor, helped him gain a deeper comprehension of business concepts and the significance of grasping opportunities.

Cuban carried on with his business endeavors during his time at college. He attended the University of Pittsburgh after high school, but after his first year, he switched to Indiana University Bloomington. Indiana's robust business program and affordable tuition were the main reasons for his decision. Cuban showed his passion for entrepreneurship while attending college by managing several modest firms. Among his noteworthy endeavors was the establishment of Motley's Pub, a bar he co-founded with many pals. Cuban oversaw the bar while still underage, gained experience in business management, and successfully traversed the difficulties of a strictly regulated sector.

Mark Cuban

Cuban relocated to Dallas, Texas, following his 1981 business administration degree from Indiana University. After working as a bartender for a while, he went on to become a sales representative for Your Business Software. His disapproval of company practices and independent tendencies made his tenure at Your Business Software brief. Cuban lost his job because he failed to open the business on time and instead closed a big sale. This failure did not discourage him but rather strengthened his will to achieve his goals.

Using his expertise in software and computer systems, Cuban established the computer consultancy company MicroSolutions in 1983. With little money when he founded the business, he was fervently committed to providing top-notch customer service. MicroSolutions expanded swiftly and provided a variety of services, such as system integration and software resale. Cuban's ability to recognize and satisfy client needs along with his hands-on approach made the company successful.

Mark Cuban

With MicroSolutions emerging as a major force in the emerging tech sector, Cuban's standing as an astute businessman started to take shape. After the business generated over $30 million in sales, Cuban sold MicroSolutions to CompuServe in 1990 for a $6 million sum. A turning point in Cuban's career was this sale, which gave him the money he needed to investigate other business opportunities and establish himself as a prosperous businessman.

Cuban's business acumen was sharpened by these early experiences; he developed a sharp sense of market prospects and an unwavering will to succeed. His journey from making trash bags into a multimillion-dollar business set the foundation for his subsequent undertakings and proved the value of perseverance, hard work, and an unwavering spirit of entrepreneurship.

The Initial Attempts

Mark Cuban

Mark Cuban's entrepreneurial journey, marked by a blend of ambition, ingenuity, and a risk-taking attitude, started at a very young age. In addition to focusing on producing money, his early endeavors also aimed to teach him the principles of business, comprehend the demands of his clients, and build resilience.

Among Cuban's first business endeavors was the sale of trash bags. He had wanted to purchase an expensive pair of basketball sneakers since he was twelve years old. He made the decision to earn the money himself rather than begging his parents for it. To purchase a large quantity of trash bags and go door-to-door in his area, he begged his father for a loan. Cuban learned several important lessons from this endeavor, including the value of hard labor, profit margins, and salesmanship. He gained knowledge on how to effectively pitch his product and handle rejection, two abilities that would come in very handy later in his career.

Cuban persisted in looking at many business ideas while still a teenager. He made money by selling coins and stamps, leveraging his passion for collecting. He had to establish contacts with other collectors, bargain over prices, and comprehend the market value of certain artifacts to succeed in this endeavor. It served as a preliminary introduction to the ideas of supply and demand, as well as the nuances of catering to clients with specialized, occasionally esoteric interests.

Cuban taught dancing as a high school student, showcasing his business spirit even more. Seeing a need among his friends, he provided disco dance lessons, which were very popular at the time. This endeavor aimed to provide a service that people want while simultaneously capitalizing on a trend to make money. It demonstrated Cuban's aptitude for seeing market demands and his readiness to venture outside of his comfort zone to satisfy them.

Cuban's aptitude for business persisted throughout his time in college. He first enrolled at the University of Pittsburgh after high school, but he quickly transferred to Indiana University Bloomington because of its excellent business curriculum and reasonably priced tuition.

Mark Cuban

Cuban started several small enterprises while attending Indiana University. Among his noteworthy endeavors was the establishment of Motley's Pub, a bar he co-founded with many pals. Cuban ran the pub while underage, gaining experience in managing a business in a heavily regulated sector. He gained knowledge in operations, customer service, and regulatory compliance from this experience.

A noteworthy endeavor he undertook while in college was a chain letter company. Cuban came up with a plan with his buddies to solicit tiny donations from people through chain letters. Even though this endeavor was brief and operated in a murky area of the law, Cuban learned the value of ethical issues in business as well as the effectiveness of direct marketing from it.

Cuban relocated to Dallas, Texas, following his time in college to become well-known in the business world. After working as a bartender for a while, he went on to become a sales representative for Your Business Software. He had a brief but significant tenure with Your Business Software. Cuban lost his job because he failed

Mark Cuban

to open the business on time and instead closed a big sale. This failure did not discourage him, on the contrary, it strengthened his determination to steer his course.

Using his expertise in software and computer systems, Cuban established the computer consultancy company MicroSolutions in 1983. Despite having little money when he founded the business, he was fervently committed to giving outstanding customer service. MicroSolutions provided a variety of services, such as system integration and software resale. Cuban's hands-on style and aptitude for recognizing and satisfying client demands contributed to the business's success. With over $30 million in revenue, MicroSolutions became a major force in the tech sector under his direction. His $6 million sale of MicroSolutions to CompuServe in 1990 was a turning point in his career.

Cuban sharpened his business instincts and acquired a good awareness of market prospects through his early ventures. His journey from making trash bags into a multimillion-dollar business proved the value of perseverance, hard work, and an unshakeable entrepreneurial spirit. All of his endeavors, no matter how minor, helped him gain a deeper comprehension of business concepts and the significance of grasping opportunities. These early encounters prepared Cuban for his subsequent achievements by demonstrating his capacity to upend the status quo and add substantial value to the business sector.

Cuban's Methodology for Small Enterprises

Mark Cuban's approach to small business is influenced by his inventive ideas, unwavering determination, and firsthand experiences. His rise from humble entrepreneurial origins to billionaire status and prominence across multiple industries provides insightful information about his tactics and worldview.

Mark Cuban

The idea of hard effort lies at the heart of Cuban's strategy. Cuban discovered early on that hard work and determination are necessary for economic success when he started out selling stamps and trash bags. He frequently stresses the need to put in the time and effort necessary to accomplish goals. Throughout his tenure at MicroSolutions, where he worked nonstop to establish the business from the bottom up and frequently went above and beyond to satisfy clients and guarantee the company's success, Cuban demonstrated this work ethic.

Additionally, Cuban emphasizes the value of knowing and attending to the needs of the client. He learned the significance of customer service from his early experiences, and he applied this concept to all of his endeavors. For instance, Cuban's dedication to offering top-notch service at MicroSolutions helped set the business apart in a crowded industry. He feels that the most important thing for every small business is to know what customers need and to go above and beyond for them. This customer-focused strategy encourages word-of-mouth recommendations and loyalty, both of

Mark Cuban

which are essential for the expansion of small businesses.

Adaptability and innovation are essential elements of Cuban's business plan. He has always been open to experimenting with novel concepts and cutting-edge technologies. His co-founding of Broadcast.com, a pioneer in internet audio and video streaming, demonstrated this forward-thinking attitude. The key to Cuban's success has been his ability to anticipate new technologies' potential and adjust to shifting market conditions. He exhorts proprietors of small businesses to keep up with market developments and to always look for new and creative methods to enhance their products and services.

Cuban also promotes the value of lifelong learning. He reads a lot and thinks that knowledge and education are essential for business success. Cuban frequently admits to reading for hours on end on a variety of subjects every day, including finance, technology, current affairs, and business trends. His dedication to education enables him to keep one step ahead of the competition and make wise decisions. Cuban's example highlights the value of lifelong learning and maintaining a sense of curiosity about the world for small business entrepreneurs.

Another essential component of Cuban's strategy for small business is financial discipline. He counsels business owners to practice financial responsibility and frugality. Living within one's means and shunning credit cards are two of his well-known pieces of advice. According to Cuban, maintaining financial discipline gives companies the flexibility to seize opportunities as they present themselves and keeps them stable through difficult times. This strategy was especially clear in his early years when he led a modest lifestyle and invested profits back into his businesses.

Cuban's strategy also emphasizes how important it is to take measured risks. Several audacious choices that paid off handsomely throughout his career stand out, such as the sale of Broadcast.com to Yahoo! for $5.7 billion in stock. Cuban is cautious about distinguishing between prudent risks and careless bets, though. He is a supporter of doing extensive study and giving important business decisions significant thought. This means that small business owners need to be ready for a range of scenarios and balance the possible rewards against the risks.

Building connections and networking are essential components of Cuban's entrepreneurial approach. He has continuously used his contacts to expand his businesses because he recognizes the importance of having a strong network. Cuban's success has been largely attributed to his capacity to establish and preserve relationships with partners, clients, and colleagues in the industry. He exhorts entrepreneurs of small businesses to actively build their networks and look for mentors and advisors who can offer direction and support.

Lastly, Cuban is a firm believer in the strength of resiliency and perseverance. His path is replete with obstacles and disappointments, from losing employment to adjusting to the ups and downs of the tech sector. Nonetheless, Cuban's success has largely been attributed to his unwavering resolve and capacity for success after setbacks. He counsels business owners to persevere in the face of difficulty, learn from their errors, and never give up.

In conclusion, Mark Cuban approaches small business with a combination of perseverance, hard effort, creativity, constant learning, financial restraint, measured risk-taking, networking, and resilience. His trajectory from hawking trash bags to constructing multimillion-dollar enterprises provides a model for would-be business owners. Small business owners can successfully traverse the difficulties of entrepreneurship and achieve long-term success by adhering to these principles.

Errors and First Teachings

Throughout his career, Mark Cuban has experienced several setbacks and learned many priceless lessons from

Mark Cuban

them. He didn't have an easy or clear route to success; instead, it took a lot of tr officials, errors, and tenacious work to become the successful businessman he is today.

When Cuban was a student at Indiana University, he had one of his first big setbacks. Continually searching for business ventures, Cuban chose to open Motley's Pub as a bar with his buddies. The project drew a sizable student audience and was initially successful. But running a bar came with responsibilities that Cuban and his partners were ill-prepared for. In addition to dealing with rowdy customers and regulatory difficulties, they also had to handle the challenges of operating a business in a highly competitive industry. The company eventually ran into financial problems and had to close. Cuban learned important lessons from this experience about the value of financial management, regulatory compliance, and an awareness of market dynamics. Following his graduation from college, Cuban relocated to Dallas, Texas, where he worked as a bartender before being hired as a sales representative by Your Business Software, a PC software firm. Cuban's unorthodox methods and independent spirit quickly caused him to run afoul of his employer. In one famous instance, Cuban neglected to open the store on time and instead closed a big sale. Even though this conduct increased income for the company, Cuban was quickly fired since it violated company rules. This humiliating experience of being fired highlighted the significance of abiding by company policies and the possible repercussions of putting short-term gains ahead of long-term relationships. But it also strengthened his desire to be his boss and his belief in the importance of business.

Cuban chose not to let this loss stop him from using his expertise in software and computer systems to launch his own company, MicroSolutions. Even though this endeavor was successful in the end, there were many difficulties in the beginning. Cuban had to start from scratch while building a clientele, contending with severe competition and limited resources. The business occasionally had trouble paying its employees, and Cuban was frequently required to work long hours and fulfill several responsibilities inside the organization. He learned from these experiences how to be resilient, how crucial it is to manage cash flow, and how important it is to wear multiple hats as a small business owner.

During the MicroSolutions era, one of Cuban's most important learning experiences was finding out that one of his workers had been embezzling company funds. This treachery served as a sobering reminder of the value of trust as well as the significance of putting robust financial controls and supervision procedures in place inside an organization. Cuban discovered the hard way how important it is to be watchful and accountable to protect a company's assets and preserve its financial stability.

Despite its eventual success, Cuban's experience with his co-founded online radio startup, Broadcast.com, has yielded many lessons. Broadcast.com underwent multiple revisions and encountered several technological and commercial obstacles. Cuban saw the tech market's volatility firsthand during the dot-com bubble. Although the dot-com bubble burst after Broadcast.com was sold

Mark Cuban

to Yahoo! for $5.7 billion in equity, the deal was a huge success and brought attention to the dangers of overvaluation and quick market expansion. Cuban learned the value of timing, market cycles, and the necessity of calculated exits during this time.

Cuban learned another important lesson from his numerous investing endeavors. Not all of the investments he made were successful. Because he participated in the television series "Shark Tank," Cuban has invested in several startups, not all of which have been successful. Some businesses collapsed because of bad management, faulty business plans, or incorrect assessments of the market. These encounters reaffirmed the significance of conducting thorough research, comprehending the subtleties of various businesses, and being aware of the risks involved in investing. They also emphasized the importance of drawing lessons from mistakes and applying those lessons to future judgments to make more informed choices.

Cuban's attitude to business has been significantly impacted by his mistakes and setbacks. They have

Mark Cuban

instilled in him the value of flexibility, the necessity of lifelong learning, and the necessity of maintaining humility and realism. He frequently stresses that experiencing failure is a necessary component of becoming an entrepreneur and that every setback offers a chance to improve. Cuban's long-term success has been largely attributed to his fortitude in the face of difficulty and his capacity to learn important lessons from his mistakes.

To sum up, Mark Cuban's early mistakes and the lessons he learned from them had a significant influence on the development of his business tactics and entrepreneurial spirit. His development as an entrepreneur has been aided by every event, from overcoming the difficulties of operating a college bar to handling financial errors at MicroSolutions and comprehending market volatility during the dot-com bubble. Cuban's narrative provides young entrepreneurs with insightful lessons on the value of tenacity, learning from failures, and constant adaptation to new difficulties.

Mark Cuban

CHAPTER 3: THE ROAD TO BUSINESS SUCCESS

Mark Cuban's path to success in business is evidence of his adaptability, strategic vision, and unwavering drive. His ascent to billionaire status and prominence in the corporate world is the result of a series of well-considered decisions, creative thinking, and an unwavering dedication to excellence.

Cuban relocated to Dallas, Texas, following his 1981 business administration degree from Indiana University. He started out doing a variety of odd jobs, such as becoming a bartender. During this time, he developed his interpersonal skills and refined his awareness of the professional world. His big break came when he was hired as a sales representative at Your Business Software, one of Dallas's first stores selling PC software.

Mark Cuban

Cuban's interest in the tech industry was sparked by this encounter, even if his time there was brief owing to a conflict with management
Cuban seemed unfazed by his departure from Your Business Software. Rather, it inspired him to launch his own company. Using the skills and connections he had developed as a software salesman, he established MicroSolutions, a computer consulting firm, in 1983. MicroSolutions offered a variety of services, such as networking solutions, system integration, and custom software development. Cuban took a hands-on approach, actively participating in all facets of the company, from customer service to sales. His commitment to providing outstanding customer service and his talent for spotting customer needs allowed MicroSolutions to quickly expand and build a devoted clientele.

MicroSolutions prospered under Cuba's direction in the cutthroat tech industry. The business gained prominence in the sector quickly by providing creative solutions and preserving a solid reputation for dependability and client pleasure. Cuban's knack for seeing trends and his dedication to staying on the cutting edge were essential to MicroSolutions' success. Cuban's business savvy and strategic vision were evident in the company's over $30 million in revenue by 1990.

One of the most important moments in Cuban's career was the $6 million sale of MicroSolutions to CompuServe in 1990. He was able to go with a sizable sum of money and the flexibility to pursue other business opportunities. But Cuban didn't sit back and take it all in. Rather, he persisted in looking for chances that matched his skills and areas of interest. His next major endeavor was co-founding Broadcast.com with Todd Wagner, another Indiana University alumnus. Cuban and Wagner were both frustrated that they couldn't watch Indiana Hoosiers basketball games in Texas, which led to the creation of Broadcast.com, which was formerly known as AudioNet. They had an idea for a platform that would allow live audio broadcasts to be streamed over the internet—a groundbreaking concept at the time. After AudioNet's 1995 launch, it soon added video streaming to its portfolio and changed its name to

Mark Cuban

Broadcast.com. The company established itself as a leader in the digital media field with its cutting-edge technology and early foray into the streaming market.

Cuban's astute strategic judgment and imaginative leadership propelled Broadcast.com's explosive expansion and success. He took advantage of the growing demand for online content as he recognized how the internet may change the way people consume media. The company's 1998 initial public offering (IPO) proved to be a huge success, as the value of its shares surged. The next year, Yahoo! bought Broadcast.com for $5.7 billion in equity, thereby turning Cuban into a billionaire. This transaction demonstrated his ability to spot and seize new trends, further solidifying his position as a leading tech entrepreneur.

Gaining notoriety and fortune, Cuban expanded his business interests and financial portfolio. The Dallas Mavericks were one of his most noteworthy purchases in 2000. The Mavericks were having difficulties on and off the court at the time, but Cuban recognized the potential in the team. His innovative thinking and hands-on style made the Mavericks a successful and well-respected NBA franchise. Cuban made investments to develop an excellent culture within the organization, improve the fan experience, and upgrade the team's facilities. The 2011 NBA Championship that the Mavericks won their first time under his ownership is proof of Cuban's astute strategic planning and capable leadership.

Cuban's investment portfolio grew to include startups, technology, and entertainment in addition to sports. In addition to starting AXS TV, a cable and satellite television network, he also co-founded 2929 Entertainment, a media firm that produces and distributes movies. His reputation as a shrewd investor and adviser to aspiring business owners was further cemented by his involvement as a "shark" on the hit television program "Shark Tank." Cuban has invested in several firms through "Shark Tank," offering not just financial support but also insightful advice and coaching. Cuban adheres to a few fundamental ideas that define his strategy for commercial success. Initially, he emphasizes the need for diligence and commitment. He thinks that

Mark Cuban

working hard and pursuing objectives with tenacity are the keys to success. Second, Cuban is a strong supporter of creativity and flexibility. He recognizes the value of keeping up with business developments and is prepared to change course when called upon. Third, knowing and satisfying the wants of customers is important to Cuban customer service. Over his career, his dedication to offering top-notch service has been a recurring theme.

Cuban's success has also been greatly attributed to his prudent risk-taking and financial self-discipline. He is renowned for his cautious evaluation of financial prospects and his thrifty approach to personal finance. Cuban is also a lifetime student who never stops learning new things and keeping up with a variety of subjects. His dedication to education enables him to keep one step ahead of the competition and make wise decisions.

In conclusion, Mark Cuban's journey to financial success is a tale of foresight, perseverance, and strategic thinking. From his early years in Dallas to his innovative forays into the tech and entertainment sectors, Cuban has continuously proven his capacity for innovation, adaptation, and leadership. His experience teaches prospective business owners important lessons and emphasizes the value of tenacity, customer focus, and ongoing education in building successful businesses.

Gaining Knowledge in Business

Mark Cuban's rise to prominence as an investor and entrepreneur is largely due to his ongoing acquisition of business acumen. His path is distinguished by a combination of formal schooling, real-world encounters, and an unwavering will to learn and adapt.

Cuban's economic aptitude was greatly influenced by his early experiences. He was involved in several side projects from an early age, including the sale of coins, stamps, and trash bags. He learned the fundamentals of profit margins, customer service, and sales through these activities. What matters most is that they taught him the importance of money and a strong work ethic.

Cuban commenced his college career at the University of Pittsburgh, where he received his official education. He did, however, quickly switch to Indiana University Bloomington because of its reasonably priced tuition and well-regarded business school. Due to Indiana University's strong business department and debt-free options, Cuban decided to attend. This choice demonstrates his early appreciation of sound financial management, a trait that would serve him well in his professional life.

Cuban threw himself into the business program at Indiana University, learning about management, marketing, and finance. He made the most of his resources by engaging fully in class discussions and building relationships with teachers and peers. During his tenure at Indiana University, Cuban developed his entrepreneurial abilities in addition to his academic knowledge. During his college years, he operated several small companies, notably Motley's Pub, a bar. Cuban gained experience in operations, regulatory compliance, and customer relations by managing the bar; this experience supplemented his academic knowledge and was quite helpful.

Cuban relocated to Dallas, Texas, following his 1981 business administration degree from Indiana University. There, he worked at several jobs to further hone his commercial acumen. His first job was as a bartender, where he honed his people skills and discovered how crucial it is to provide a satisfying experience for customers. Even though it had nothing to do with his long-term objectives, this employment helped him better grasp hospitality and service.

As a sales representative for Your Business Software, a company that offered PC software, Cuban had his first notable professional position. His career took a significant turn when he was hired, as it introduced him to the rapidly growing tech sector. Cuban developed his sales abilities at Your Business Software, where he learned how to make product pitches, close deals, and negotiate terms. Additionally, he developed a stronger grasp of the software industry and the technical requirements of companies. Even though he had a falling out with management when he left Your Business Software, the experience had a significant impact on how he approached business.

In 1983, following his dismissal from Your Business Software, Cuban launched MicroSolutions, his own business. This choice signaled the start of his entrepreneurial career. Cuban oversaw all facets of the company at MicroSolutions, including marketing, sales, technical assistance, and customer care. He was compelled to swiftly acquire a broad range of business abilities due to this all-encompassing responsibility. He gained knowledge of financial management, which includes financial forecasting, cash flow management, and budgeting. Cuban also developed strong networking skills, which were essential for MicroSolutions' expansion as he forged connections with customers, vendors, and colleagues in the field.

Mark Cuban

Cuban was especially notable for the way he handled customer service at MicroSolutions. He thought that to create enduring, solid relationships with his clients, great service was essential. By emphasizing customer happiness, MicroSolutions was able to stand out in a crowded field and set the stage for future growth. Cuban's commitment to comprehending and satisfying client needs came to define his business style.

Cuban received $6 million for the sale of MicroSolutions to CompuServe in 1990, which gave him the money he needed to investigate other business opportunities. However, it was his ongoing acquisition of commercial acumen that allowed him to take full advantage of these changes. Along with Todd Wagner, he co-founded Broadcast.com, one of his most important businesses. AudioNet, the original name of Broadcast.com, was a pioneer in online audio and video streaming. The company's success was largely due to Cuban's ability to understand the potential of this technology and his willingness to take measured risks.

Mark Cuban

Cuban had to broaden his skill set even further to operate Broadcast.com. He had to oversee intricate technological advancements, manage a growing staff, and negotiate the quickly changing IT scene. Broadcast.com's supremacy in the streaming media sector may be attributed in large part to Cuban's strategic vision and leadership. Cuban's 1998 initial public offering (IPO) showed his capacity to carry out a winning business plan. The ensuing $5.7 billion sale of Broadcast.com to Yahoo! in 1999 demonstrated his aptitude for closing high-stakes agreements and figuring out when to leave a company.

Cuban's involvement on the television program "Shark Tank" as an investor and coach is another example of his refined financial acumen. As a "shark," Cuban reviews a broad variety of business presentations, which calls for him to swiftly determine whether various business ideas are viable, comprehend the workings of the market and spot possible dangers and opportunities. His success on "Shark Tank" is a testament to his command of business principles and his capacity to offer astute advice to budding business owners.

Mark Cuban

Cuban has stressed the value of lifelong learning throughout his career. He reads a lot and keeps up with a lot of subjects, from finance and technology to current affairs and business trends. His dedication to education enables him to keep one step ahead of the competition and make wise decisions. Cuban's curiosity and adaptability have proven invaluable in managing the dynamic corporate environment.

To sum up, Mark Cuban's acquisition of business acumen has been a complex process that encompasses formal schooling, real-world experiences, and an unwavering quest for knowledge. His early endeavors, education, and practical experience in a range of industries have given him a broad and strong skill set. Cuban's success as an investor and entrepreneur has been largely attributed to his capacity for innovation, adaptation, and lifelong learning. These qualities provide important takeaways for anyone aspiring to be successful in the business world.

Mark Cuban

MicroSolutions

Mark Cuban's first significant business endeavor was MicroSolutions, which was crucial in making him a prosperous entrepreneur and trailblazer in the technology sector. MicroSolutions was a computer consulting firm that was founded in 1983 and offered a variety of services, such as networking solutions, system integration, and bespoke software development. Through this project, Cuban demonstrated not only his technical prowess but also his capacity to recognize market needs and provide top-notch customer service.

Not long after Cuban lost his position at Your Business Software, MicroSolutions was born. While losing his job was unfortunate, it gave Cuban the motivation he needed to go it alone. Equipped with the expertise he had acquired in the software sector, Cuban recognized a chance to found a business that would assist companies in navigating the challenges posed by cutting-edge computer technologies. With little money when he

Mark Cuban founded MicroSolutions, he had a clear vision for offering superior technical solutions and unrivaled customer support.

Cuban ran MicroSolutions out of a modest apartment in Dallas, Texas, at the beginning. At first, the business concentrated on offering installation and support services in addition to retailing gear and software. Cuban had a close involvement in all facets of the company, including marketing, sales, technical assistance, and customer support. He was able to comprehend the nuances of the industry and make sure that each client received individualized care because of his hands-on approach.

The success of MicroSolutions was largely due to Cuban's dedication to comprehending and satisfying client needs. He felt that establishing enduring relationships with customers required offering outstanding customer service. This focus on the needs of the customer allowed MicroSolutions to stand out from the competition and swiftly develop a devoted clientele. To guarantee that customers received the most care possible, Cuban personally answered a large number of the company's sales and support calls. His commitment to client satisfaction became a pillar of the MicroSolutions brand.

The technical know-how of Cuba was yet another important asset for MicroSolutions. His in-depth knowledge of software and computer systems allowed him to provide clients with creative solutions. Cuban was constantly searching for new technology that would help his clients and enhance their business processes. With this innovative approach, MicroSolutions was able to remain ahead of industry trends and provide clients with state-of-the-art solutions. Businesses trying to improve efficiency and optimize operations particularly valued Cuban's ability to combine various platforms and create new software solutions.

Additionally, financial management was essential to MicroSolutions' expansion. Cuban took great care in overseeing the business's finances, making sure that spending was kept in check and cash flow was closely watched. He was aware of the significance of maintaining financial discipline, particularly for a startup company with little funding. MicroSolutions was able to grow its clientele and service offerings by reinvesting revenues back into the company through prudent financial management.

Cuban assembled a small group of devoted experts who shared his devotion to quality and customer service as MicroSolutions expanded. By creating a vibrant and cooperative work atmosphere, he inspired his staff to solve customer challenges creatively and proactively. Although Cuban was a hands-on manager, he also gave his staff members the freedom to own their work and make a positive impact on the business. This strategy contributed to the development of a solid team that was essential to MicroSolutions' expansion.

A significant turning point in MicroSolutions' development was landing contracts with big clients, like government organizations and multinational enterprises. These agreements gave MicroSolutions a consistent flow of income and enhanced its reputation as a major participant in the IT sector. Cuban's capacity to network and cultivate connections with influential figures played a pivotal role in obtaining these prominent contracts. His track record of providing dependable and efficient solutions enabled MicroSolutions to gain the confidence of significant clients and increase its market share.

An important factor in the early adoption of networking technology was also MicroSolutions. As companies realized how crucial computer networks were to enhancing productivity and communication, Cuban established MicroSolutions as a pioneer in networking solutions. The organization assisted organizations in making the switch to networked settings by offering complete services, such as network design, installation, and support. Clients greatly appreciated Cuban's knowledge in this field, and MicroSolutions gained a reputation for putting together dependable networking solutions.

Larger organizations in the tech industry eventually became interested in micro-solutions due to its expansion and success. MicroSolutions was purchased by CompuServe, a significant online service and software provider, in 1990 for a sum of $6 million. Cuban's career reached a major turning point with this transaction, which gave him access to large financial resources and confirmed his ability to succeed as an entrepreneur. Cuban's future triumphs were made possible by the sale of MicroSolutions, which also gave him the freedom to invest in other businesses and look into fresh prospects.

When thinking back on his tenure at MicroSolutions, Cuban has frequently highlighted the value of perseverance, hard effort, and a customer-focused mindset. The knowledge he gained during this time served as the basis for his later business endeavors and financial investments. Cuban's involvement with MicroSolutions strengthened his convictions about the importance of offering top-notch customer service, staying abreast of technology developments, and practicing cautious financial management. His success has been largely attributed to these ideas across a variety

Mark Cuban

of fields, including media, technology, sports, and entertainment.

Finally, MicroSolutions was a pivotal point in Mark Cuban's career as an entrepreneur. His technological proficiency, business savvy, and persistent dedication to customer service were all highlighted by the organization. Cuban made MicroSolutions a thriving and well-respected business by working hard, being innovative, and putting the interests of his clients first. His attitude to business has been influenced by the knowledge and abilities he gained during this time, which has contributed significantly to his sustained success as an investor and entrepreneur.

Important Obstacles and Successes

Several setbacks and victories along the way have shaped Mark Cuban's career as a millionaire

Mark Cuban

businessman. His tale is one of tenacity, cunning, and the capacity to seize chances in the face of adversity.

The choice to transfer from the University of Pittsburgh to Indiana University Bloomington was one of Cuba's first big obstacles. He made the transfer because he wanted to register in a more respectable and reasonably priced business school. Deciding to start over and leave behind a familiar surrounding was not without risk. But in the end, it turned out to be a smart decision. Cuban became fully involved in business courses and entrepreneurial endeavors while attending Indiana University, where he acquired important knowledge and experience that would eventually influence his career.

Finding his foothold in the working world was another significant obstacle Cuban had to overcome after earning a business administration degree from Indiana University. He started doing odd jobs after moving to Dallas, Texas, including bartending. Working as a sales representative for Your Business Software was his first meaningful professional position. Despite his ability to drive sales, Cuban's time at the company was short-lived

Mark Cuban

as he was dismissed for concluding a contract rather than opening the store on schedule. This setback served as a sobering reminder of the value of following corporate policies and striking a balance between immediate rewards and long-term job stability.

Cuban, unfazed by this defeat, used it as a springboard to launch the computer consulting firm MicroSolutions. There were several difficulties in MicroSolutions' early years. Due to his limited funding, Cuban was forced to run the company out of a tiny flat. He oversaw every facet of the business, including customer care, technical assistance, and sales and marketing. Despite these obstacles, Cuba's commitment and practical style enabled MicroSolutions to expand quickly. His emphasis on comprehending and satisfying client needs enabled the business to stand out in a crowded market and develop a devoted clientele.

Cuban's 1990 $6 million sale of MicroSolutions to CompuServe was one of his greatest career victories. Cuban gained substantial financial resources from this profitable exit, which also confirmed his abilities as an entrepreneur. But it also brought with it a unique set of difficulties. Cuban, who became wealthy overnight, had to learn how to manage his sudden wealth and make wise financial choices. His future triumphs were made possible by his adept handling of this change.

Broadcast.com, Cuba's next big project, had both tremendous successes and troubles. Initially known as AudioNet, a platform for live audio broadcasting online, Broadcast.com was co-founded by Todd Wagner. The business had to overcome several technological and commercial obstacles because streaming media was still a relatively new sector with lots of unknowns. In addition to overcoming financial obstacles, Cuban and Wagner had to start from scratch to grow their user base. When Broadcast.com went public in 1998 and its shares skyrocketed in value, their tenacity paid off. The ultimate victory came in 1999 when Yahoo! paid $5.7 billion in equity to acquire Broadcast.com, thereby turning Cuban into a billionaire.

Mark Cuban

Although the sale of Broadcast.com was a huge success, it also brought attention to the tech market's instability. The dot-com bubble's eventual collapse highlighted the dangers of overvaluation and quick market expansion. Cuban learned a lot about timing, market cycles, and the significance of calculated exits during this time. Notwithstanding the wider market difficulties, Cuban's ability to weather this storm and pull out at a premium enhanced his standing as an astute businessman.

Cuban experimented across several industries and diversified his assets with his newly acquired fortune. The Dallas Mavericks were one of his most noteworthy purchases in 2000. The Mavericks presented a serious challenge at the time since they were having both on-and off-court difficulties. Cuban turned the Mavericks into a successful and well-respected NBA franchise with his innovative and hands-on style. He made investments in the team's facilities, the fan experience, and the development of an excellence-oriented culture throughout the company. The 2011 NBA Championship victory by the Mavericks under his ownership was a

Mark Cuban

testament to Cuban's astute leadership and astute strategic planning.

Outside of athletics, Cuban experienced setbacks and victories in the media and entertainment sectors. In addition to starting AXS TV, a cable and satellite television network, he also co-founded 2929 Entertainment, a media firm that produces and distributes movies. Cuban had to handle the intricacies of the entertainment sector, such as content creation, distribution rights, and audience interaction, for these endeavors. His accomplishments in these domains proved his capacity to modify his business acumen for various sectors and spot new prospects.

Cuban's appearance on the television program "Shark Tank" as an investor and coach is another example of his capacity to overcome obstacles and succeed. As a "shark," Cuban assesses a broad variety of company proposals, necessitating his rapid assessment of the viability of various business ideas and his ability to recognize opportunities and hazards. Cuban has been able to invest in and advise several budding businesses because of this position. His success on "Shark Tank" is a testament to his command of business principles and his capacity to offer insightful counsel.

Cuban has had to deal with problems involving legal troubles and public criticism during his career. Being a well-known businessman and public figure, he has been involved in several scandals and court cases. For example, the Securities and Exchange Commission (SEC) launched a protracted investigation against Cuban due to claims of insider trading involving the sale of his stock in a firm named Mamma.com. Cuban vehemently refuted the accusations and was ultimately found not guilty of any of them. This event made clear how crucial it is to abide by the law and the dangers associated with making large financial decisions.

In summary, Mark Cuban's career has been shaped by several significant setbacks and victories that have shaped his path as an investor and businessman. From his early days of founding MicroSolutions to the enormous success of Broadcast.com, Cuban has proven to be resilient, astute, and able to seize chances when faced with challenges. His achievements with the Dallas Mavericks, his forays into the entertainment business, and his appearance on "Shark Tank" all serve to emphasize his capacity to overcome difficult obstacles and pull off noteworthy victories. Cuban's life narrative serves as an example of the value of tenacity, flexibility, and never-ending education in achieving long-term success.

The CompuServe Sale

One of the turning points in Mark Cuban's entrepreneurial career was the sale of MicroSolutions to CompuServe, which gave him his first significant financial success and served as a platform for his subsequent business endeavors. This deal demonstrated his capacity to start from scratch and grow a business to

Mark Cuban

a profitable exit, while also validating his business acumen.

Cuban established MicroSolutions in 1983 as a computer consulting business, and it expanded rapidly to become a major force in the IT sector. The business offered a variety of services, such as networking solutions, system integration, and custom software development. Cuban's hands-on style and commitment to client pleasure were essential in building a devoted clientele and propelling the business's expansion. MicroSolutions grew both in services and clientele under his direction, showcasing Cuban's aptitude for strategic thinking and successful business management.

By the late 1980s, MicroSolutions had become a significant success, generating large annual revenues. Large enterprises and governmental organizations were among the company's notable clientele, drawn by its reputation for providing inventive and dependable solutions. The IT industry took note of this achievement and was interested in purchasing MicroSolutions due to its well-established market presence and knowledge.

Mark Cuban

Among these interested parties was CompuServe, a well-known supplier of software and online services. CompuServe was aiming to bolster its position in the quickly changing tech industry and broaden its product offerings at the time. It was a compelling offer to purchase a business with the track record and solid clientele of MicroSolutions. The acquisition was a wise move for both businesses because MicroSolutions' offerings and CompuServe's strategic goals aligned. MicroSolutions and CompuServe engaged in a complex negotiation process that included valuing MicroSolutions' assets, client contracts, and market potential with great care. Cuba played a pivotal role in the negotiations. His in-depth knowledge of MicroSolutions' business and value proposition allowed him to successfully negotiate a good agreement. Cuban's ability to negotiate and his financial acumen were crucial in obtaining a substantial purchase price that accurately represented the worth of the firm he had founded from the ground up.

Mark Cuban

One of the biggest moments of Cuban's career was the $6 million sale of MicroSolutions to CompuServe in 1990. For Cuban, this transaction was both a financial boon and an endorsement of his business endeavors. Cuban received a sizable amount of capital from the deal, which he used to finance his next projects, including Broadcast.com. With the sale's financial certainty, Cuban was free to explore new avenues and take calculated chances without worrying about short-term financial restraints.

Within the larger framework of the technology sector, the MicroSolutions sale brought to light several significant patterns and processes. It highlighted how crucial system integration and computer consulting services were becoming at a time when companies were embracing computers more and more. The acquisition was also indicative of the IT industry's consolidation trends, as bigger firms like CompuServe looked to strategically acquire other businesses to expand their capabilities.

Mark Cuban

Acquiring MicroSolutions was a calculated decision for CompuServe that complemented its expansion goals. CompuServe was able to incorporate MicroSolutions' proficiency in software development and system integration into its service portfolio through the acquisition. CompuServe's ability to offer comprehensive solutions to its clients was strengthened as a result, solidifying its position in the market. The strategic significance of the acquisition was proven by CompuServe's operations through the integration of MicroSolutions' capabilities.

From an entrepreneurial standpoint, there were three key takeaways from the sale of MicroSolutions. It first emphasized how important it is to have a solid basis for customer satisfaction and high-quality service in business. Cuban's dedication to comprehending and satisfying client needs plays a significant role in MicroSolutions' success and appeal to potential investors. Second, the sale made clear how crucial market positioning and strategic thinking are. The expansion and ultimate acquisition of MicroSolutions were greatly aided by Cuba's ability to spot and seize new trends in the tech sector.

Furthermore, the CompuServe acquisition of MicroSolutions showed how entrepreneurs might make significant financial gains by strategically selling their companies. This deal functioned as a model for other business owners who wanted to create and dissolve profitable enterprises. It also emphasized how important it is to secure a contract that accurately represents the value of the company and how important negotiation skills are.

Building and selling MicroSolutions was a transforming experience for Cubans. It gave him the money and self-assurance he needed to go after bigger, more audacious projects. The knowledge gained at this time regarding negotiating, strategic expansion, financial management, and customer service persisted in shaping Cuban's business philosophy in the years that followed. His other endeavors, such as the immensely popular Broadcast.com, were founded upon the knowledge and understanding he acquired while working at MicroSolutions.

In conclusion, Mark Cuban's career took a significant turn when he sold MicroSolutions to CompuServe. It was his first significant business success and served as a platform for other endeavors. The deal demonstrated Cuban's capacity to establish and grow a company, engage in successful negotiation, and secure a profitable exit. CompuServe's market position and service offerings were improved by the acquisition. Important lessons about customer satisfaction, strategic expansion, and the possibility of financial success through the strategic sale of a corporation were demonstrated by the MicroSolutions transaction. This historic occasion shaped Cuban's outlook on business and his subsequent accomplishments, paving the way for his ongoing success as an investor and entrepreneur.

Mark Cuban

Getting Started in Broadcasting

With his daring moves and well-timed investments, Mark Cuban changed the media landscape and cemented his status as a visionary businessman upon his entry into the broadcasting sector.

Cuban's involvement with the broadcast industry started in 1995 when he co-founded Broadcast.com, which was then known as AudioNet. Cuban saw the potential for audio material streaming on the internet at a time when it was developing quickly. Cuban founded AudioNet with business partner Todd Wagner to offer live web streaming of radio stations, athletic events, and other audio content. Cuban's first entry into the broadcasting sector, this project paved the way for his future media and entertainment ventures.

As one of the first companies to use streaming video technologies, Broadcast.com immediately became well-known. Cuban and Wagner profited from the increased demand for real-time audio material as well as the popularity of the Internet. They got deals to stream content online from radio stations, big sports leagues, and entertainment companies. Thanks to its strategic posture, Broadcast.com has been able to develop a wide range of audio offers that appeal to a wide range of sports fans, music lovers, and news consumers.

Several important reasons contributed to Broadcast.com's success. Cuban's in-depth knowledge of media and technology trends allowed the business to keep one step ahead of rivals and take advantage of new opportunities in the digital sphere. During his time at MicroSolutions, he used his knowledge of software development and system integration to create a stable streaming platform that could support numerous concurrent users and provide high-quality audio content online.
Additionally, Cuban's business acumen was very important to Broadcast.com's expansion. Acknowledging the revolutionary possibilities of streaming media

technology, he made calculated investments to enhance the organization's potential. To expand Broadcast.com's content collection, Cuban concentrated on improving user experience, making investments in technology infrastructure, and forming alliances with content producers.

The 1998 initial public offering (IPO) of Broadcast.com was a turning point in the company's history. The IPO was a huge success, demonstrating investor faith in streaming media's future and solidifying Broadcast.com's position as a major player in the tech sector. On the first day of trade, the company's shares shot up, propelling Cuban and Wagner into the public eye as forward-thinking businessmen. Additionally, Broadcast.com received a sizable amount of funding from the IPO to further develop its business and look for fresh growth prospects.

Another significant accomplishment for Broadcast.com came in 1999 when Yahoo! purchased the company for $5.7 billion in equity. The transaction, which at the time was among the biggest in internet history, solidified Cuban's standing as a cunning businessman and pioneer in the broadcasting sector. Yahoo!'s purchase of Broadcast.com demonstrated the strategic importance of the business's content distribution and streaming technologies.

Cuban kept up his strategic investments in the entertainment and broadcasting industries after Broadcast.com was sold. He is one of the co-founders of HDNet (now AXS TV), a cable and satellite television network that specializes in live sporting events, entertainment shows, and music performances. Offering high-definition programming at a time when HD television was becoming more and more popular with viewers was one way that HDNet set itself apart.

Cuban's broadcasting aspirations were significantly influenced by his ownership of the Dallas Mavericks. The Mavericks gained a reputation under his direction for adopting cutting-edge fan experiences and utilizing digital media to interact with fans. To improve the Mavericks' brand and fan engagement tactics, Cuban

Mark Cuban

made investments in digital content creation, interactive fan experiences, and cutting-edge arena technology.

Apart from his broadcasting endeavors, Cuban has been a strong proponent of media and entertainment's future. He has advocated for the adoption of technological innovations, like digital distribution platforms and streaming media, to adapt to changing customer demands and market conditions. Because of his understanding of how media and technology are combined, Cuban is now regarded as a thought leader in the field.

In conclusion, Mark Cuban's foray into the broadcast industry was distinguished by his astute grasp of media and technological trends, as well as his entrepreneurial vision and well-timed investments. His co-founding of Broadcast.com changed the online distribution and consumption of audio content and helped to establish the streaming media sector. The triumph of Broadcast.com, which resulted in Yahoo! purchasing it!cemented Cuban's standing as a trailblazer in the internet and broadcasting industries. His other endeavors—such as

Mark Cuban

HDNet and his ownership of the Dallas Mavericks—further show his power and impact on the entertainment and media industries. Through his financial contributions, astute observations, and support of technological advancements in digital media, Cuban remains a dynamic force determining the broadcast industry's destiny.

Mark Cuban

CHAPTER 4: BILLION-DOLLAR SUCCESS

Mark Cuban's path to billion-dollar success crosses several business endeavors and sectors, demonstrating his strategic vision, entrepreneurial spirit, and capacity to seize new opportunities in media and technology.

Yahoo! and Broadcast.com Acquisition

One of the pivotal events in Cuban's career was when he and Todd Wagner co-founded Broadcast.com, then known as AudioNet, in 1995. Acknowledging the possibilities of internet-based media streaming, Cuban and Wagner established Broadcast.com as a trailblazing platform for real-time audio streaming, encompassing radio stations, athletic events, and other entertainment content.
During the dot-com boom, Broadcast.com swiftly rose to prominence and was among the top suppliers of

streaming media technologies. Cuban's strategic leadership and profound knowledge of technology trends made it possible for the business to form alliances with prominent media, entertainment, and sports leagues. This increased the amount of content available on Broadcast.com and drew a sizable user base, solidifying the company's position as the industry leader in digital media.

One of the most anticipated and profitable initial public offerings (IPOs) of the year, Broadcast.com made news in 1998 with its successful IPO. The IPO confirmed investor faith in streaming media's future and elevated Wagner and Cuban to the status of visionary businessmen. With the help of the money raised from the IPO, Broadcast.com was able to significantly expand its platform and improve its technological infrastructure.

When Yahoo! purchased Broadcast.com in 1999 for $5.7 billion in equity, the company reached its zenith of success. The acquisition cemented Cuban's position as a billionaire businessman and was a historic agreement in the history of the Internet. Hurray! acquired Broadcast.com, demonstrating both the strategic significance of the business's streaming technology and content distribution capabilities and Cuban's ability to identify and seize on new digital trends.

Ventures at Post-Broadcast.com

After Yahoo! purchased Broadcast. com, Cuban kept going for business endeavors in a variety of sectors, solidifying his billion-dollar success:

- Dallas Mavericks Ownership: Cuban acquired the bulk of the NBA team, the Dallas Mavericks, in 2000. The Mavericks saw a revival both on and off the court during his ownership. In 2011, Cuban's creative fan interaction strategy, player development investments, and dedication to creating a winning culture helped the Mavericks win their first NBA Championship. Under Cuban's direction, the Mavericks were successful, which further cemented

Mark Cuban

his standing as a revolutionary in the world of professional sports ownership.

Media and Entertainment Ventures: Cuban was a co-founder of HDNet (now AXS TV), a cable and satellite television network that specialized in high-definition sports events, live music performances, and entertainment programming. HDNet sets itself apart from the competition by providing premium content and excellent viewing experiences to a discriminating audience seeking cutting-edge viewing technologies.

- Investments and Entrepreneurial Ventures: Cuban has made calculated bets on several technological businesses in addition to media and sports. He is well-known for his work as an investor on the TV show "Shark Tank," where he coaches budding business owners and assesses their pitches. Cuban's investment portfolio is vast and reflects his experience as a venture capitalist. It includes investments in consumer goods, technology, healthcare, and digital media, among other industries.

Mark Cuban

The Philosophy and Impact of Entrepreneurship

Cuban has advocated a daring entrepreneurial attitude marked by creativity, risk-taking, and an unwavering pursuit of greatness throughout his career. He stresses the significance of keeping up with industry developments, comprehending market dynamics, and adjusting to technology breakthroughs. In addition to his financial sense, Cuban's success as a millionaire entrepreneur is a result of his capacity to recognize bright prospects, forge important alliances, and efficiently utilize his resources.

Cuban's influence goes beyond his own business endeavors and financial investments. He is an outspoken supporter of education, entrepreneurship, and the advancement of technology. Through his writings, interviews, and public appearances, Cuban regularly offers his opinions and suggestions on leadership, corporate strategy, and economic trends. His stature in the business world and beyond highlights his position as a mentor and thought leader for budding business owners who want to follow in his footsteps.

In summary, Mark Cuban's path to billion-dollar success is evidence of his visionary leadership, astute strategic planning, and enterprising nature. From the early days of the internet boom, when he founded Broadcast.com, to turning the Dallas Mavericks into an NBA champion and making significant investments in a variety of businesses, Cuban has continuously shown that he can innovate, adapt, and prosper in cutting-edge markets. His legacy as a multibillionaire investor and entrepreneur continues to influence and mold global entrepreneurship and digital innovation.

Knowledge Acquired from the Dot-Com Boom

Mark Cuban

Mark Cuban gained insightful knowledge and significant lessons from his experience during the dot-com bubble, which influenced his philosophy of investment, entrepreneurship, and business management. Fast expansion and speculation in internet-related stocks and businesses defined the dot-com bubble, which peaked in the late 1990s and early 2000s. Being one of the most well-known businessmen of the time, Cuban experienced both highs and lows during this tumultuous time, learning personally about the workings of the market, risk management, and the value of sustainable business methods.

1. Realistic Assessment

For Cubans, one of the most important takeaways from the dot-com bubble was the significance of fair pricing. Many IT companies and internet startups were valued more on potential during the boom than on hard metrics like revenue, profitability, or steady development. As a result of the speculative valuation, stock prices rose, and many businesses eventually failed as investors realized they would not receive the expected returns.

Cuban highlights the need to evaluate a company's or technology's intrinsic value before making an investment or depending only on market hype or forecasts for the future. He supports a methodical approach to valuation that takes into account qualitative as well as quantitative variables, making sure that investments are supported by reliable financial theories and reasonable development projections.

2. Pay attention to sustainability and cash flow.

A crucial lesson that Cuba took away from the dot-com bubble was the significance of managing cash flow and maintaining financial stability. Many dot-com businesses prioritized quick growth and gaining market share above building a strong base for revenue generation and profitability. When funding dried up or investor opinion changed, this strategy proved unsustainable and resulted in widespread financial problems and bankruptcies.

Mark Cuban

Cuban highlights that companies must put profitability, operational effectiveness, and cash flow management first from the beginning. He thinks that to achieve sustainable growth, investment, spending, and revenue creation must be balanced. Cuban's emphasis on sound financial management techniques and discipline is a reflection of his dedication to creating companies that are strong enough to weather market ups and downs.

3. Risk management and diversification

The dot-com bust brought to light how crucial risk mitigation and diversification are to investing portfolios. Cuban saw directly how concentrated holdings in tech stocks—high-risk, high-reward—could result in large losses during bear markets. He discovered that to reduce risk and protect money, it is important to diversify assets over a range of businesses, asset classes, and geographical areas.

Mark Cuban

Cuban supports a diverse portfolio made up of a variety of stocks, bonds, real estate, and alternative assets. By reducing exposure to the volatility of individual stocks or industries, diversification helps disperse risk. Because he saw the negative effects of excessive risk-taking and speculative investing during the dot-com bubble, Cuban's approach to risk management is influenced by these experiences.

4. Pay attention to market fit and customer value.

Cuban discovered the value of concentrating on market fit and customer value from a business standpoint. Numerous dot-com businesses ignored consumer needs or had a poor understanding of their target market in favor of expansion at all costs. This method frequently produced client acquisition plans and business models that were not scalable or long-term viable.

Cuban is an advocate for companies to put market validation, product innovation, and customer pleasure first. According to him, the foundation of a successful

Mark Cuban

business is providing clients with real value and consistently adjusting to the demands of the market. Long-term growth and sustainable competitive advantages can be built by firms through customer-centric approaches, product and service iterations, and listening to customer feedback.

5. Flexibility and Originality

Ultimately, Cuban learned from the dot-com bubble the value of creativity and adaptability in managing shifting market conditions. After the bubble burst, several prosperous companies arose by modifying their business plans, incorporating new technologies, and improving their strategy. Cuban thinks that even in difficult economic times, tenacious businesspeople are prepared to change course, try out novel concepts, and seize fresh chances.

Cuban's professional path demonstrates his dedication to lifelong learning, flexibility, and creativity. After seeing

Mark Cuban

early success with Broadcast.com, he expanded his investments into several different sectors, such as sports, media, technology, and entertainment. Cuban has been able to maintain his entrepreneurial success and influence in the international business community by being open to embracing technological improvements, investigating new business opportunities, and questioning traditional wisdom.

To sum up, Mark Cuban learned a great deal about risk management, financial sustainability, value realism, customer focus, and adaptability from his experiences during the dot-com bubble. His approach to corporate leadership, investment techniques, and entrepreneurial philosophy have all been influenced by these teachings. Cuban's understanding of the dot-com era still influences his support for ethical entrepreneurship in a constantly changing global marketplace.

Mark Cuban

Increasing Investment Diversification

Through a variety of industries and asset classes, Mark Cuban's approach to investment diversification reflects his strategic vision, philosophy of risk management, and entrepreneurial agility. Cuban has accumulated a sizable investment portfolio that includes holdings in technology, media, sports, entertainment, and other industries through a combination of active involvement, calculated purchases, and diverse portfolio management.

1. Investments in Technology

Cuban's investment approach in this field has been shaped by his early achievements and technological expertise. He actively looks for chances in disruptive breakthroughs, scalable business strategies, and new technology. Cuban makes investments in a variety of technology companies, from start-ups in their early stages to well-established businesses with promising future growth and creative solutions.

His IT investments frequently center on fields including software development, digital media, cybersecurity, and artificial intelligence. Cuban can recognize promising firms and technologies that have the potential to upend entire sectors thanks to his insights into consumer behavior and technology trends. Using his background as an investor and entrepreneur, he helps tech firms overcome obstacles and seize market opportunities by offering mentorship and strategic advice.

2. Entertainment and Media

Cuban's media and entertainment endeavors demonstrate his dedication to investing in a variety of industries that share his enthusiasm for content production, distribution, and customer interaction. He is a co-founder of HDNet (now AXS TV), a cable and satellite television network that specializes in high-definition sporting events, live music performances, and entertainment programs.

Mark Cuban

Through this business, Cuban was able to serve a niche market seeking premium content and improved watching experiences while utilizing his skills in broadcasting and digital media.

Cuban investigates stakes in streaming services, online entertainment, and digital content platforms in addition to traditional media. He understands how customer tastes for tailored experiences, interactive media, and on-demand content are changing. Cuban's investments in this field are intended to take advantage of changes in consumer behavior and technical developments that will influence how media is consumed in the future.

3. Athletics and Entertainment

Cuban is the owner of the Dallas Mavericks, an NBA team, and has made large investments in entertainment and sports. His ownership of the Mavericks combines his business savvy with his love of basketball to create a strategic investment in professional sports. Under

Cuban's direction, the Mavericks have become a prosperous team renowned for its creativity, involvement from fans, and community service.
Cuban investigates investments in esports, sports analytics, and sports technology in addition to basketball. He acknowledges the increasing impact of technology on media rights, fan interaction, and sports performance. Cuban invests in sports-related businesses to profit from the confluence of sports and entertainment, data analytics, and digital transformation trends.

4. Final Goods and Services

A wide variety of consumer goods and services that adapt to shifting customer tastes and lifestyle trends are included in Cuba's investing portfolio. He looks for opportunities in the retail, hospitality, health & wellness, and consumer technology industries. When making investments in consumer goods, Cuban frequently emphasizes market scalability, brand distinction, and innovation.

Mark Cuban

Through his involvement in consumer goods startups, Cuban can assist business owners who are creating cutting-edge solutions to satisfy the needs of their target market. To help entrepreneurs achieve market success and speed expansion, he offers access to his network of industry contacts, operational skills, and strategic guidance. Cuban's investments in this industry are a reflection of his optimism about consumer-driven companies' ability to upend established marketplaces and generate value for all parties involved.

5. Alternative Assets and Real Estate

Cuban allocates cash to real estate and alternative assets that provide long-term growth potential and diversification advantages to diversify his investment portfolio. He makes investments in income-producing assets that offer chances for both capital appreciation and steady cash flow, as well as in residential and commercial real estate.

Mark Cuban

Cuban looks at investing in alternative assets like venture capital funds, cryptocurrency, and blockchain technology in addition to real estate. He sees these alternative investments as chances to take advantage of new developments in technology and finance, diversify risk, and protect against market volatility. Cuban's attitude to alternative assets is indicative of his openness to investigate prospects for non-traditional investments that could yield substantial returns and diversify a portfolio.

6. Strategic Investment Methodology

Cuban's investment technique has been typified by diligent due diligence, proactive portfolio management, and a disciplined approach to risk management throughout his career. He stresses how crucial it is to keep up with changes in the market, business, and economic factors that affect investment choices. Due to his active involvement in his investment portfolio, Cuban can successfully evaluate prospects, manage risks, and take advantage of market opportunities.

Mark Cuban

Mark Cuban's strategy for diversifying his investments is a reflection of his adaptability as an entrepreneur, his strategic vision, and his dedication to creating a portfolio that is diverse and spans a variety of asset classes. His investments in consumer goods, technology, media, sports, real estate, and alternative assets demonstrate his proactive approach to investment diversification and wealth management. Cuban continues to influence the global business community and serve as an inspiration to aspiring investors and entrepreneurs thanks to his investment expertise and track record of success as an entrepreneur.

Mark Cuban

CHAPTER 5: DISRUPTING INDUSTRIES

Through audacious investments, creative endeavors, and inspiring leadership, Mark Cuban has made a name for himself as a disruptive force across a variety of industries. His entrepreneurial trajectory is distinguished by his unwavering quest for innovation, his readiness to question received wisdom and his dedication to using technology and wise investments to revolutionize several industries.

1. Broadcasting and Media

Cuban has had a significant influence on the media and broadcasting sector, especially as a result of his innovative work in digital content distribution and streaming media. When Cuban co-founded Broadcast.com (then known as AudioNet) in 1995, he saw the unrealized promise of audio content delivery via

Mark Cuban

the Internet. The platform immediately rose to prominence as a top source of live streaming for radio stations, entertainment shows, and sporting events.

The historic 1999 acquisition of Broadcast.com by Yahoo! for $5.7 billion was the result of the site's success, demonstrating the strategic importance of content aggregation and streaming media technologies. Cuban transformed the media landscape by using his abilities to capitalize on new internet trends and his vision for digital content delivery, which laid the groundwork for the ongoing digital streaming revolution.

2. Entertainment and Sports

Cuban has revolutionized the sports and entertainment industries as the owner of the Dallas Mavericks, an NBA team, by bringing a fresh perspective to franchise ownership and fan interaction. The Mavericks have adopted technology under his direction to boost player performance, increase fan experiences, and increase organizational effectiveness.

Mark Cuban

Cuban's commitment to using technology to spur innovation in sports administration and entertainment is demonstrated by his investments in esports, sports analytics, and sports technology. He has put the Mavericks at the vanguard of sports technology innovation by investing in firms that emphasize data-driven decision-making, athlete performance enhancement, and fan involvement.

3. Startups and Technology

Cuban has had a significant influence on the technology sector that goes beyond his early success with Broadcast.com. By making wise investments in startups and cutting-edge technologies, he keeps up his disruptive and influential work in the technology field. Among the businesses in Cuban's investment portfolio are those engaged in software development, digital media, cybersecurity, and artificial intelligence.

Mark Cuban

He uses his experience as an investor and entrepreneur to find innovative companies and game-changing technology that could completely change entire sectors. The development and prosperity of creative businesses in the technology sector are facilitated by Cuban's active participation in business mentoring, strategic advice, and industry connections.

4. Goods and Services for Consumers

Cuban's investments in consumer goods and services demonstrate his dedication to funding businesses that provide creative answers to the wants and needs of customers. He looks for business possibilities in the consumer technology, hospitality, retail, health and wellness, and health and wellness sectors. He concentrates on brands that stand out from the competition with innovative products and scalable markets.

Through his participation in consumer product businesses, Cuban can assist business owners in creating and introducing cutting-edge goods that appeal to consumers. Understanding consumer behavior, adjusting to market trends, and providing value-driven solutions that upend established markets are all crucial components of Cuban's investment strategy.

5. Venture Capital and Entrepreneurship

Cuban's impact as a disruptor extends beyond certain industries, as evidenced by his support of venture capital and entrepreneurship. Cuban is a well-known investor on the television show "Shark Tank," where he assesses business proposals, coaches budding entrepreneurs, and makes investments in cutting-edge companies with room to develop. His influence as an investor and mentor has increased as a result of his work on the show, encouraging business owners to pursue their ventures and overcome obstacles.

Cuban's investment philosophy and entrepreneurial path are a reflection of his faith in the ability of technology, innovation, and strategic thinking to upend markets and spur economic expansion. He has established himself as a pivotal role in business and entrepreneurship thanks to his capacity to spot possibilities, reduce risks, and seize new trends. Cuban's record as a visionary investor and entrepreneur influencing the direction of international markets is further highlighted by his ongoing dedication to upending industries and encouraging innovation.

Technology and Media

Due to his successful business endeavors, astute investments, and inspirational leadership in revolutionizing the production, distribution, and consumption of information, Mark Cuban has had a profound impact on the media and technology industries for many years.

Early Broadcasting Attempts

Mark Cuban

Along with Todd Wagner, Cuban founded Broadcast.com (formerly known as AudioNet) in 1995, marking the beginning of his career in media and technology. Cuban was the first to introduce the idea of audio streaming via the Internet, seeing the potential of the Internet to transform media distribution. Radio shows, sporting events, and other digital content can all be streamed live on Broadcast.com, which rose to prominence very fast.

The triumph of Broadcast.com demonstrated Cuban's vision of utilizing cutting-edge technologies to upend established media structures. During the dot-com boom, his focus on providing real-time content online positioned Broadcast.com as a leader in the streaming media space. Cuban's standing as a tech visionary was cemented by the company's 1998 initial public offering (IPO) and 1999 acquisition by Yahoo! for a sum of $5.7 billion. These events highlighted the strategic importance of digital content delivery.

Effect on Content Distribution and Digital Media

Mark Cuban

Beyoncé's impact on digital media transcends his initial triumph with Broadcast.com. Through his investments in online media projects, streaming services, and digital content platforms, he continues to influence the digital environment. Businesses at the vanguard of digital innovation, such as those in social networking, digital advertising, video streaming, and content creation tools, are part of Cuban's investment portfolio.

His deliberate investments in digital media are a reflection of his faith in the revolutionary potential of technology to democratize the production and consumption of content. Cuban is a promoter of consumer-centric media consumption strategies that place a focus on interactive participation, on-demand access, and individualized content experiences. To profit from changes in consumer behavior toward digital platforms and mobile-first content consumption, he invests in digital media firms.

Athletic and Recreational Activities

Mark Cuban

Cuban's influence on the nexus of sports, entertainment, and technology has been further cemented by his ownership of the Dallas Mavericks of the NBA. The Mavericks have adopted technology to boost player performance, improve fan experiences, and increase operational efficiency under his direction. Cuban's commitment to using technology to spur innovation in sports administration and entertainment is demonstrated by his investments in esports, sports analytics, and sports technology.

Apart from the Mavericks, Cuban has made investments in sports-related firms that concentrate on fan interaction platforms, sports media content, and athlete performance optimization. His interest in sports technology is a reflection of his optimism about how digital innovation and data-driven decision-making might transform the sports sector.

Promoting Innovation and Entrepreneurship

Mark Cuban

Apart from his commercial endeavors, Cuban is a strong proponent of digital literacy, innovation, and entrepreneurship. Through his blog, media appearances, and public speaking engagements, he frequently provides his thoughts and advice on industry trends, startup growth methods, and upcoming technology. Cuban supports entrepreneurship even in his capacity as an investor on the television show "Shark Tank," where he assesses and counsels prospective business owners.

Cuban's dedication to encouraging creativity, invention, and disruption in the digital era has defined his influence on media and technology. His business path from Broadcast.com to trailblazing digital media investments showcases his aptitude for spotting emerging markets, spotting game-changing technologies, and seizing chances that will influence media consumption and technological advancement in the future.
Mark Cuban's impact on media and technology highlights his significance as a revolutionary force in the digital age. Digital media, content distribution, and sports technology are all being advanced by his business

Mark Cuban

endeavors, astute investments, and support for innovation. Cuban's legacy as a media disruptor and tech visionary demonstrates his unwavering dedication to using technology to make a significant influence on international markets and sectors.

Mark Cuban

CONCLUSION

Cuban has pushed the envelope of what is conceivable, disrupted conventions, and exemplified disruption throughout his career. His initial forays into software sales and consulting established the foundation for his trailblazing involvement in the internet revolution with Broadcast.com, which in the end transformed the online distribution and consumption of media material.

Beyond his savvy in business, Cuban's ownership of the Dallas Mavericks has been distinguished by his dedication to quality, inventiveness in sports administration, and love of creating a winning environment. Not only have the Mavericks been successful on the court under his direction, but they have also emerged as a role model team renowned for their community service and fan interaction.

Mark Cuban

Cuban's reputation as a shrewd businessman ready to support and train up-and-coming entrepreneurs has been further cemented by his role as a "shark" investor on the popular television program "Shark Tank". Numerous business owners have been motivated to follow their passions and upend entire sectors by his risk-taking and frank advice.

When we consider Cuban's path from Pittsburgh to the highest levels of business and athletics, it's impossible not to be impressed by his fortitude, foresight, and steadfast faith in the potential of creativity. In addition to shaping his success, his readiness to accept change and question the status quo has inspired countless people to think boldly and take decisive action.

More than just a biography, "Mark Cuban: Disrupting the Status Quo - From Garbage Bags to Billions" is a monument to the lasting legacy of a man who never stops innovating and inspiring. Cuban's narrative serves as a reminder that everything is possible if you have passion, tenacity, and the willingness to disrupt things as we look to the future.

www.ingramcontent.com/pod-product-compliance
Lightning Source LLC
Chambersburg PA
CBHW071943210526
45479CB00002B/788